Original title:
The Caregiver Chronicles

Copyright © 2025 Creative Arts Management OÜ
All rights reserved.

Author: Ronan Whitfield
ISBN HARDBACK: 978-1-80581-782-6
ISBN PAPERBACK: 978-1-80581-309-5
ISBN EBOOK: 978-1-80581-782-6

Unspoken Promises of Care

In the land of endless laundry,
Where sock monsters roam free,
I chase the crumbs and spilled milk,
With a wipe that's as brave as me.

With a smile that's stretched too thin,
I juggle snacks and bedtime tales,
For every toddler tantrum,
A hero's laugh prevails.

In a world of sticky fingers,
And crayons on the wall,
I find joy in the chaos,
With stumbles that make me tall.

So here's to all the mishaps,
And moments filled with glee,
For in each little giggle,
There's magic, wait and see!

Echoes of Empathy

In a world where chaos reigns,
One sock is lost, oh where it wanes!
Juggling snacks, with spills and drops,
While laughter echoes as the chaos hops.

A superhero with messy hair,
Waging battles with kitchenware.
From crayons strewn to toys afloat,
They navigate this wild boat.

Hands of Healing

A hand that soothes a skinned-up knee,
A magic potion brewed with glee.
Band-aids sparkly, and kisses too,
Turning tears to giggles, who knew?

In the chaos of the daily grind,
A moment's rest is hard to find.
But oh, the joy in tiny wins,
As lullabies chase away the spins.

Shadows of Tenderness

In the shadow of a bedtime quest,
A glass of water—a toddler's test.
Monsters under the bed, oh dear!
They giggle at shadows, never fear.

Giggles ignite in morning's light,
As breakfast battles take to flight.
Pancakes as frisbees in joyful flight,
What a way to start the day bright!

Threads of Solace

In tangled yarn, a cozy mess,
A knit cap made in happiness.
With laughter woven into each row,
Love's comfort grows, just watch it flow.

A painted handprint on the wall,
A canvas of chaos, a sweet brawl.
Each thread a story, a moment caught,
In this tapestry, joy is sought.

A Tapestry of Touch

With gentle hands and silly hats,
I juggle spoons and dance with cats.
A tickle here, a pat on back,
We laugh while plotting our next snack.

Each hug a stitch in life's great thread,
We weave our joy, no room for dread.
In chaos, there's a choreographed spree,
Just me and my wild circus, carefree!

Banana peels and flying pies,
When laughter fills the air, who cries?
We share our tales with clumsy flair,
In this tapestry, joy's everywhere!

So bring your quirks and join the fun,
Life's a show, we're never done.
With smiles and giggles, we'll embrace,
This colorful world, a loving space.

Heartbeats in Harmony

Bouncing balls and clattering spoons,
Dancing to the music of silly tunes.
With each heartbeat, a funny cheer,
   We celebrate life, let out a jeer.

Putting mismatched socks on our feet,
   Each step's a waltz, a goofy beat.
We shuffle and slide, no need for grace,
   In this vibrant, silly race!

Pillows as thrones and giggles abound,
In our kingdom of joy, we are crowned.
We may trip, but we'll never fall,
   In harmony, we stand tall!

Our laughter with the stars will play,
As heartbeats dance the night away.
Together we thrive, a joyful crew,
   In perfect sync, just me and you.

Through Fragile Eyes

With curious glances and a cheeky grin,
What silly tales to let the fun begin?
Through fragile eyes, a world so bright,
Where every mishap becomes delight.

We trip on clouds and dance with bees,
In this topsy-turvy world, we tease.
Each little blunder a story to tell,
In our whimsical universe, all is swell.

From jelly spills to shoe lace fights,
Our days are painted in goofy sights.
Glances exchanged like secret codes,
In laughter, we travel down funny roads.

Through delicate lenses, we'll navigate,
This carnival of joy, we celebrate.
Together, we'll craft a glorious mess,
In fragile sights, we find our best!

Stories in Solitude

In cozy corners with mismatched chairs,
We spin our yarns with giggles and stares.
Solo adventures in a bubbly mind,
Where imagination dances, unconfined.

Talking to shadows, embracing the light,
Silly dialogues that spark delight.
With each quiet chuckle, we find our muse,
In the whimsical world, there's no excuse.

Comical tales of noodles and pies,
Laughter echoing under starry skies.
Every secret shared, a giggly boon,
In solitude, we croon to the moon.

So gather your quirks, let stories unfold,
In a symphony of laughter, be brave and bold.
With silly whispers as our guiding tune,
In stories of solitude, fun shall bloom!

The Heart's Embrace

With hugs and snacks at hand,
They dance through the day,
Telling jokes no one will understand,
In a fun, silly way.

A stethoscope around their neck,
They walk with a skip,
Turning every ache to a speck,
On the humor-filled trip.

With band-aids in the kitchen drawer,
And glitter on their shoes,
They mend hearts and spirits galore,
While cracking all the blues.

In every smile and playful jest,
They turn pain into cheer,
For healing, they are simply the best,
With laughter as their spear.

Beneath the Stethoscope

Underneath the stethoscope,
Lies a world of cheer,
Where laughing's more than just a trope,
And joy is always near.

With charts and cupcakes piled high,
They juggle and they laugh,
Mixing medicine with a pie,
In their own silly gaffe.

Instead of gloom and heavy sighs,
They sprinkle fun like spark,
Turning frowns to brightened skies,
Amidst their vibrant spark.

With witty quips and funny face,
They bring warmth to the room,
For in this lively, special place,
There's always room to bloom.

Chronicles of Kindness

In the tales of everyday,
Laughter takes the stage,
With a sprinkle of joy at play,
To help turn every page.

They've got band-aids and warm soup,
And tickle fights on cue,
Creating a big, happy troupe,
To brighten up the view.

Every problem's just a jest,
Every sigh, a new joke,
In this saga, we're all blessed,
With smiles that never choke.

From silly hats to wild dance moves,
Kindness takes the lead,
In this world that always grooves,
Laughter's our only creed.

Lanterns in the Dark

With lanterns bright, they light the way,
Through the shadows of the night,
Where giggles guide us, come what may,
In a world that feels just right.

They bring the fun to every call,
With humor in their stride,
Turning stumbles into a ball,
Where laughter's the true guide.

With whispers soft and antics slick,
They chase away despair,
In every smile, a little trick,
No sadness left to share.

So here's to those who find the spark,
In moments of the bleak,
For they are true, our little lark,
The laughter that we seek.

Harvesting Hope

In the garden of dreams, we plant,
A little bit of laughter, a little bit of chant.
Watering with joy, we pull weeds of despair,
Who knew we'd find sunshine, hidden under a chair?

Every seed that we sow, a tale it will tell,
Of mishaps and giggles, and friends that fell.
With a bucket of patience and a trowel of grace,
We grow smiles so bright, they can light up a space.

Chronicles of Care

In the world of the silly, we take on our tasks,
Juggling soap bubbles while wearing our masks.
With capes made of laughter and shoes filled with cheer,
We navigate chores, although we may veer.

Every call for assistance, a chance for a jest,
Who needs a superhero? We've got the best!
With each heartfelt hug and the joy that we share,
Our chronicles weave fun in the art of care.

Songs of Solitude

In a moment of quiet, a tune fills the air,
The dance of the dust bunnies, beyond all compare.
With a whisk as the mic, and a mop as the band,
We sing to the rhythm of our own little land.

In solitude's corner, we laugh at the mess,
An orchestra of one, in this grand little quest.
While the clock ticks in tempo, we sway and we glide,
It's a ballet for one, where the giggles won't hide.

The Gift of Presence

With a sprinkle of kindness and a dash of delight,
We show up for each other, from morning to night.
Our presence, a present, wrapped up tight with glee,
Who needs fancy gifts when you've got good company?

In the chaos of chaos, we find the calm beat,
Like dancing with shadows on our two happy feet.
Embracing the madness, with chuckles we share,
It's the gift of our presence that shows that we care.

Worn-out Shoes and Warm Hearts

In shoes so worn, we chase the day,
With giggles bright, we find our way.
Coffee spills and laughter rings,
Who knew joy came from little things?

A sock that's lost, a shoe that's stained,
Yet every mishap leaves us entertained.
With muddy footprints, we paint the floor,
Each step a story, who could ask for more?

Through giggles shared and snacks we stash,
The clock just laughs as we make a dash.
With arms full of hugs, we march along,
In worn-out shoes, we sing our song.

So here's to days that fill our hearts,
Where laughter's loud, and joy imparts.
Amidst the chaos, love's always near,
In worn-out shoes, life's full of cheer.

The Light in Their Eyes

A wink, a smile, a playful tease,
Moments like these are sure to please.
With mischief wrapped in twinkling gaze,
We dance in circles, a joyful maze.

Bright lights twinkle where shadows dwell,
Catching stories too sweet to tell.
In every laugh, a glimmer shines,
With playful puns and clever lines.

In the chaos, we find our swings,
With joyful chaos, the heart just sings.
Like little stars that flicker and soar,
The light in their eyes keeps us wanting more.

So let's ignite joy on the longest nights,
Unwrap the laughter and cast the lights.
With hearts so full and spirits high,
In memories made, we learn to fly.

Letters to the Lonely

A crumpled note, a silly rhyme,
A joke about pets or a dance-off time.
Ink spills like laughter across the page,
Gifts of giggles, a laugh-filled stage.

With stickers here, and drawings there,
We send our love, crafted with care.
A reminder that silliness is key,
To brighten the world, just wait and see.

So if you feel blue or lonely tonight,
Just check your mailbox, oh what a delight!
For in those letters, joy finds a way,
To chase all your worries far, far away.

Let's write our tales, full of joy and cheer,
With goofy sketches, we've nothing to fear.
For the magic of laughter lives in our ink,
And in the warm notes, we'll always shrink.

Moments Behind the Mask

Behind the mask, a wink peeks through,
With playful secrets shared by the few.
Silly faces in a mirror's glare,
Laughter escapes from everywhere.

As giggles bounce off walls so bright,
We dance and twirl, hearts taking flight.
With every mask, a story unfolds,
Of joy and silliness yet to be told.

Who knew behind this fabric disguise,
Lay merry moments and joyful cries?
In silly poses and funny stares,
We find the love that's always there.

So put on your mask, let's make it grand,
In every moment, together we stand.
With laughter's echo, we'll share with glee,
For joy is the mask that sets us free.

The Soul's Salve

In a busy ward, humor reigns,
With jokes that dance like playful trains,
Band-aids donned like superhero capes,
Healing smiles and funny shapes.

Coffee spills and laughter bright,
Mismatched socks, a silly sight,
Thermometers turned to candy canes,
Oh, laughter—what a joyous gain!

A dance of wheelchairs down the hall,
Each wobble made—a giggly sprawl,
In this circus of care, we jest,
Finding humor is truly the best!

When tears burst forth, we crack a pun,
Bringing warmth like the sun,
In moments tough, we play the fool,
In laughter's light, we often rule.

Unraveling Layers of Grief

Sometimes grief wears a funky hat,
With polka dots and a friendly chat,
Underneath, we joke and tease,
Touching hearts like a warm breeze.

Tissues fly like confetti in the air,
Laughter bubbles, freeing despair,
With every giggle, we find escape,
Lightening burdens—no need for a cape.

Memories dance in silly ways,
Reminding us of brighter days,
A trip down memory lane—oh dear!
The past can laugh, it's safe here!

From sorrow's depths, we rise with glee,
Clowns in the sadness, merrily!
Finding humor is our shared gift,
In the wreckage, we still lift.

Care Beyond Compare

With a wink and grin, we navigate,
Through the wilds of elder fate,
A dance with meds, a jig with care,
Who knew love could be so rare?

We swap old tales, a minstrel's play,
With giggles rolling, night to day,
In our hearts, we cherish it all,
Humor that always stands tall.

Cookbooks filled with ingredients odd,
Salads made with a friendly nod,
Oh, those times we cook and burn,
Teaching each other with lessons learned.

Every hug's a magic spell,
Turning tears into stories to tell,
In this journey, we find our way,
With laughter brightening each day.

In the Company of Hearts

In a room full of stories and sighs,
We bounce around like balloons in the skies,
Colors swirling, a lively affair,
Laughter echoes; it fills the air.

Silly hats and mismatched shoes,
Life's quirks are our muse,
We spin yarns of adventures grand,
In this merry, loving band.

With a belly laugh and playful tease,
Comfort flourishes with such ease,
We play with words to banish dread,
Creating joy where once was lead.

In moments stitched with laughter bright,
We find our way through the night,
Each heartbeat shared, a joyful start,
In this love, we play our part.

The Pulse of Presence

In a world that spins, I'm here with cheer,
Juggling tasks while I sip my beer.
Laughter echoes through the halls,
As I trip over toys and loose small balls.

With a smile so wide, I serve up a snack,
Turning chaos to fun, never looking back.
With stories of dragons and magic in air,
I brandish my spatula, without a care.

Bedtime's a circus, with giggles in tow,
As I wrestle with blankets, putting on a show.
While tucking in secrets, and checking for fears,
I might just get caught in my own happy tears.

Kindness in Action

An old dog snoring, a cat on my lap,
I bring snacks for all, hear their cheerful clap.
With sticky hands and splattered paint,
I wear my apron, a true work of quaint.

Through the chaos, kindness blooms like a flower,
Sharing all laughter, in every hour.
They claim I'm a legend, a superhero in disguise,
But really, I'm just good at stealing fries!

From playdates gone wrong, to dances in rain,
I manage the madness, and all the sweet pain.
With hugs that heal, and kisses that stick,
Life's a comedy show, and I'm the top pick!

Gentle Footprints

Tiny footprints trailing all through the house,
Searching for snacks, as quiet as a mouse.
With giggles and whispers, they sneak all around,
Hiding in corners, not making a sound.

"Dinner's not ready!" I call with a grin,
As they race for the cookies, my patience wears thin.
But their laughter echoes, and I can't help but beam,
This wild, funny journey is truly a dream.

Catching memories in all shades of joy,
From mischief to magic, not just for a boy.
With gentle footprints, my heart's been set free,
In a world made of giggles, oh, come dance with me!

Bridges of Understanding

In a land made of stories spun wild and strange,
We build bridges of laughter, always ready to change.
With crayons and laughter, we color our day,
Turning frowns into giggles, come what may.

Preparation for chaos, I've got my degree,
In chocolate-covered hugs and tea parties, you see.
Through whispers of magic and silly debates,
We navigate rivers of fun, oh, it's never too late!

When tempers flare high, we just reach for the snacks,
A diversion of cookies, and all's back on track.
With bridges of understanding, love glows from afar,
In this joy-filled adventure, we're all shining stars.

Guardian of Grace

In a world of chaos, I find my flair,
With mismatched socks, and wild hair.
I dance through spills like a pro,
Dodging toys like a ninja, you know.

With a cape made of laundry, I save the day,
From tantrums and snacks in a clever way.
I wield a spatula, my trusty sword,
Cooking meals that are slightly adored.

Tangles in hair, a battle I face,
Each morning routine, a wild goose chase.
I chuckle at chaos, a laugh in my throat,
As I treasure each moment, my joy, my antidote.

So here's to the giggles and messes we make,
A life full of laughter, no chance for a break.
With love as my armor, I embrace each race,
In this whirlwind of life, I'm the guardian of grace.

The Language of Love

In a world where nonsense makes perfect sense,
I speak in giggles, my secret defense.
With every hug, I translate the mood,
Even if my dance moves are somewhat crude.

I read the signs from a glance or a sigh,
Like a translator with donut in eye.
Every whimper and whisper, I know what it means,
Even when it's hidden under ice cream machines.

Words are overrated, I strut with a song,
With funny faces, we laugh all day long.
My heart's a balloon that's ready to pop,
With bouncy intentions that never will stop.

So dance with my chaos, my love, my best mate,
In this silly language, we celebrate fate.
Through giggles and grins, let's soar like a dove,
In the heart of the whirlwind, we speak the language of love.

Beneath the Surface

Beneath the surface, where chaos may roam,
Lies a world filled with joy, and a little grime home.
Here socks go missing, and spoons disappear,
Yet treasures are found in the giggles we share.

With crayons on walls and wild paint on clothes,
I tiptoe through puddles where laughter just flows.
A zoo made of stuffed toys, they all have their names,
Whispering secrets in giggly refrains.

The dirt on my jeans, a badge of pure love,
I'll wear it with pride; it fits like a glove.
Underneath all the chaos, a spark always shines,
In the mess of our moments, the best love defines.

So life is a circus, a grandiose show,
Where laughter's the thread that we masterfully sew.
Beneath all the surface, in fun we'll dive deep,
Through silliness, joy, our bond we will keep.

Navigating the Labyrinth

In the labyrinth of toys, we wander and weave,
Decoding the pathways, it's hard to believe.
With a snack in my pocket and hope in my stride,
I navigate mazes where giggles collide.

Lost in the tangle of pillows and beds,
I dodge every trap, with lightness it spreads.
The map is in crayon, a riddle to crack,
With twisty routes leading us forward and back.

Each corner I turn, there's a treasure concealed,
A half-eaten cookie where laughter is healed.
Notes made of giggles are all that I need,
In this maze of love, I'm destined to lead.

So here's to the journey, the twists and the bends,
In the heart of this labyrinth, where laughter extends.
Through every detour and playful surprise,
We'll navigate together, under giggly skies.

Symphony of Support

In the chaos, we dance a jig,
With snacks in hand, we laugh so big.
Mismatched socks and silly hats,
Life's a circus, with love that chats.

We juggle tasks with a pie in the face,
Finding joy in our wild embrace.
Fumbling words, and all that fun,
Together we shine like the bright sun.

The dog steals fries, the cat plays too,
Our home's a zoo, with a laughing crew.
With every stumble, we giggle loud,
In this crazy love, we are so proud.

So here's to us, the quirky bunch,
With every hug and every munch.
In this symphony of care and cheer,
We make magic, year after year.

Grace Among the Nurtured

With a smile that could light the night,
Spilled juice becomes a funny sight.
We tread on toys, our feet they squeak,
In this ballet of love, we're far from bleak.

Mismatched schedules dance around,
Like a comedy show, our joy is found.
In the chaos, we waltz, oh so spry,
It's all a part of our lullaby.

Diapers tossed like confetti bright,
We laugh 'til tears blur our sight.
Each tiny laugh a sweet reward,
Through trials and tumbles, we feel adored.

In every moment, we embrace the mess,
With grace and giggles, we feel so blessed.
For in the journey, we find our place,
In the art of love, we find our grace.

Portraits of Resilience

Here's a picture of our wild ride,
With paint and glitter, it's hard to hide.
Crayons broken, colors spill,
In this masterpiece, laughter is our thrill.

Each stumble leads to a funny pose,
Our lives a gallery of crazy shows.
With sticky hands and smiles so wide,
Through every challenge, we take it in stride.

A snapshot of chaos, a sprinkle of fun,
Our hearts connect 'til the day is done.
We frame our memories in shades of cheer,
In every laugh, our love draws near.

Portraits of resilience hang on the wall,
Through laughter and tears, we embrace it all.
In this gallery of heart, forever we'll stay,
Creating a masterpiece, day after day.

The Weight of a Shoulder

When the world feels heavy and quite absurd,
A shoulder to lean on is the craziest word.
With laughter's lift, we share the load,
In this wild journey, our love is bestowed.

Balancing chores like a circus act,
With a wink and a grin, that's a fact.
Two left feet on a dance floor of care,
In every misstep, joy fills the air.

We trade our worries for silly pranks,
Through every challenge, we fill the blanks.
With a giggle and hug, we lighten the way,
In this shoulder dance, we save the day.

So here's to the moments we weave with glee,
With the weight of the world, just you and me.
In this playful embrace, we find our strength,
Together we soar, no matter the length.

Universes of Understanding

In a world of Band-Aids and hopes,
We navigate the slippery slopes.
With coffee cups and laughter loud,
We turn chaos into a crowd.

From missing socks to minor spills,
Our missions fueled by caffeine thrills.
With jokes that soar like paper planes,
We can fix hearts, ignore the stains.

With stethoscopes and silly games,
We'll save the day and share the names.
Each hug a prescription, each cheer a cure,
In this universe, our hearts are pure.

So here's to jests in our care zones,
Cooking up empathy with silly tones.
We gather strength from funny quirks,
In every smile, our purpose works.

The Quiet Strength

In hugs so tight, strength is found,
In whispers soft, love's profound.
While juggling tasks like circus clowns,
We wear our hearts, not frowns.

Amid the hurry, time takes flight,
We're dancing through the day and night.
With playful jabs and cheeky grins,
Our caring ways always wins.

We patch the wounds with laughter and flair,
A sprinkle of joy in the air.
With unspoken bonds that tightly mesh,
We turn our day into comfort fresh.

Through all the mess, we find our groove,
Quiet strength in every move.
So here's to love, with a wink and a jest,
In the art of caring, we are truly blessed.

Whispers of Compassion

In the corners where problems loom,
We find the light in every room.
With chocolate bars and silly pranks,
We turn those frowns into laughs and thanks.

With whispered words, like bubbles rise,
We craft a world with joyful sighs.
Each tear we catch, a badge we wear,
Compassion laced in playful flair.

A spilled drink? Just more giggles poured,
In this house of love, we won't be bored.
From stories told in high-pitched tones,
To playful teasing through our phones.

So let's embrace the tender jest,
In every heart, we give our best.
With whispers soft, our laughter flows,
In the garden of care, compassion grows.

Silent Sutures

With bandages and scrapes, we are quite the crew,
Stitching laughter where the pain once grew.
With puns like penicillin, we heal the sore,
In the quiet nights, we find so much more.

While sutures sit quietly in trays,
We craft our night into clever plays.
With every slip, we share a grin,
In the art of care, we always win.

In secret smiles and knowing looks,
We dive into life like open books.
Our laughter echoes under the moonlight,
In every silence, our hearts feel light.

So raise a toast to fun in the fray,
For every moment brings a brighter day.
With silent sutures and a flair for fun,
In the dance of care, we've already won.

The Path Less Traveled

In slippers worn, I make my way,
Through snacks and toys that like to play.
A detour here, a mount of socks,
There's treasure everywhere—forgotten rocks.

Each corner turned, a surprise awaits,
A squirrel, a shoe, or mismatched plates.
Oh, how I wander! A life unplanned,
With hearts and laughter, hand in hand.

The cat gives chase, the dog takes flight,
My to-do list? It vanished from sight.
As giggles echo through the hall,
I think perhaps I've got it all.

So here's to paths that twist and sway,
Where laughter lives and rules the day.
Next time you frown at chores in sight,
Just take a step—make it a flight!

Pillars of Resilience

With every fall, I learn to stand,
A pile of laundry, a sticky hand.
Each spill a story, every sigh a song,
In this chaos, I somehow belong.

My coffee's cold, my patience thin,
But oh, the joy beneath the din.
Like a circus juggler, I'm on a spree,
With children, pets, and chaos all around me.

The messier the house, the louder the cheer,
For every tantrum brings a new frontier.
Pillars built not from brick or stone,
But from giggles shared and love we've sown.

So raise your cups—let's toast today!
To laughter and love in disarray.
With every trial, we'll stand tall,
Together we rise, together we fall.

Beneath the Weary Surface

Beneath the weary, a spirit bright,
Hiding away from morning light.
With cereal spills and hair askew,
Each day feels strange, yet oddly new.

As socks take wing and toys parade,
My inner zen begins to fade.
But in the chaos, a dance appears,
With silly moments that drown my fears.

We laugh by day, we snore by night,
Through tangled dreams, we'll find our flight.
In loving stumbles, we embrace the ride,
For in the silly, we find our guide.

So let's be merry as we tease the fuss,
With joy and giggles, ride the bus.
Beneath the weary, the sparks ignite,
In the heart of care, we find our light.

Cradled in Care

Cradled in care, where whispers bloom,
With endless hugs that chase the gloom.
Dinosaurs dance, while fairies fly,
In our little world, we start to sigh.

The puppy's antics steal the show,
As we giggle at his playful glow.
In crayon art and rambunctious play,
We celebrate life in our own way.

From bedtime tales that twist and weave,
To morning chaos that we believe.
Each mischief makes our hearts expand,
As laughter lingers, hand in hand.

So here's to moments we hold so dear,
In cradled arms, it's love we steer.
Amidst the frenzy, joy takes flight,
In playful hearts, we lose the fight.

Sheltering Souls

In a house that's filled with glee,
Socks and shoes are one, you see.
A spoon is missing, oh what luck,
Found in the dog's new toy truck.

Pancakes stacked up, tall and wide,
Butter flies off, it takes a ride.
'Breakfast is served!' I cheerfully shout,
But the cat thinks it's a time to pout.

The laundry calls, a mountain high,
Lost another shirt, oh my, oh my!
The puppy's paw, a worked-out mess,
Came in muddy, yes, I confess.

But laughter echoes, we're one big team,
Tangled in chores, living the dream.
With silly faces and playful jive,
In this chaos, we thrive and strive.

Lanterns of Love

Tickle fights in the bright moonlight,
Shadows dance, oh what a sight!
With pillows as shields, we set our stage,
Pretending we're knights, it's all the rage.

The cookies burned? A crunchy treat!
"Just adds texture!" we laugh and eat.
In mismatched socks, we cha-cha slide,
Our living room, the ultimate ride.

A science experiment gone astray,
Exploding soda? Hey, let's play!
Bubbles in hair, it's a messy affair,
We look like art, do we really care?

Lanterns glowing, brightening our night,
In this wild journey, hearts take flight.
With every giggle and silly game,
These little moments are never the same.

Chronicles Written in Tears

A toy train track, all set to go,
But wait! It's stuck, oh no, oh no!
With teamwork strong, we haul and heave,
In this grand saga, we both believe.

A lost shoe causes a drama queen,
"Where's the other?!" a frantic scene.
But laughter bubbles through each tear,
This is our story, loud and clear!

The goldfish jumped, oh what a splash!
Water everywhere, it's quite the crash!
With towels thrown like capes of cheer,
We save the fish, and we persevere.

In chronicles penned with cartons and glue,
Every mishap brings a laugh anew.
Through silly struggles, our bond grows tight,
In this whirlwind, we find pure delight.

The Ray of Relief

A mess of toys sprawled on the floor,
Who needs a gym? This is better for sure!
Dodging legos in the dim light,
Each tiny step, like a ninja fight.

Suddenly silence, a moment so rare,
What's brewing up, oh where, oh where?
A secret concoction, rainbow surprise,
Sticky fingers, and glittery eyes.

With spoons and pots, we start a band,
Playing to rhythms, it's totally unplanned.
From crazed tambourines to a loud drum beat,
Our kitchen concert, oh man, what a feat!

But when the hour grows late and the stars appear,
We end each day with a smile and a cheer.
In these moments of chaos and glee,
We find our home, harmonious and free.

Moments of Solace

In the chaos of a toddler's mess,
A sock found in the cereal press,
Laughter bursts like bubbles in air,
As I wonder how a shoe's in there.

With crayons coloring the wall so bright,
I question why art isn't black and white,
Amidst the giggles and the sticky hands,
My sanity dances in unlikely bands.

To spot a binky beneath the couch,
Turns my heart into a joyful vouch,
While toys conspire in a grand parade,
And peace is just a snack away made.

In those odd moments of sweet delight,
I find my muse in the tireless fight,
A chaotic ballet, a comic reel,
Here's to every reckoning we feel.

Guardians of the Unseen

In the land of lost socks and sticky floors,
We wield our mops like mighty swords,
Battling crumbs that staged a coup,
While two-year-olds giggle and squeal 'woo-hoo!'

The bedtime saga, oh what a spree,
Researching where the plush lion could be,
With a flashlight under the bed, we shout,
'Who needs sleep when there's fun about?'

Late-night whispers turn to raucous roars,
As the monsters shiver behind bedroom doors,
With a cape of blankets, we take a stand,
Guardians of dreams in this sleep-deprived land.

We laugh through the mishaps, the rants, and the plays,
In this whimsical world, we spend our days,
For every giggle that rings in the night,
Makes the crazy battles ever so bright.

Echoing Empathy

A toddler's tears splash like summer rain,
I can't help but laugh at their little pain,
With each dramatic fall to the floor,
There's wisdom in chaos, oh, let's explore!

In the art of sharing, we're always in luck,
'Til two chocolate bars lead to quite the cluck,
Negotiations break down over just one bite,
Yet laughter replaces the fussing in sight.

Through imaginative tales of pirates and wands,
We navigate messes like well-versed ponds,
With empathy echoing through each silly tale,
I find comfort in giggles when things derail.

On this quirky journey, we flourish and thrive,
In the land of the lost where we strive to survive,
For every teardrop, a smile I'll forge,
In this wacky adventure, my heart's on a gorge.

A Symphony of Care

A symphony plays with pots and pans,
As kids conduct wild and witty plans,
With each clang and clatter of wooden spoons,
We sway to the beat of our joyful tunes.

In the kitchen chaos, we stir up delight,
With a sprinkle of magic, baking feels right,
Each cupcake's frosted with love and a cheer,
And laughter makes all the calories disappear!

Like a tug-of-war with laundry's embrace,
I chase the socks in this hilarious race,
For laughter's the currency we cherish and hold,
As we weave warm memories like threads of gold.

In this orchestral swell of each playful day,
We dance through the bumps and giggle away,
In the music of life, my heart beats in sync,
As I savor the moments and pause for a wink.

Fragile Moments

In a world full of giggles, winks, and sighs,
Lives a juggler of chaos with a twinkle in her eyes.
Laundry's cascading like a colorful flood,
Yet somehow she walks with grace, or at least muddled.

Bedtime stories that often go wrong,
As pets steal the spotlight, they sing a new song.
With mismatched socks on her feet, she'll twirl,
In this circus of life, she's the queen of the world.

The kitchen's a battlefield, dishes take flight,
"Who's hungry?" she yells, "Let's see what's tonight!"
Pasta a sculpture, perhaps abstract art,
But laughter erupts, and that's just the start.

When kids' antics take over and choices get lean,
She crafts silly games, like a well-laid routine.
In fragile moments, hilarity thrives,
As love and laughter keep everyone alive.

Strong Hearts

With hands that can soothe and a heart made of gold,
She navigates storms, yet never feels cold.
A superhero's cape made of laundry and hugs,
Her laughter, a potion that softens the shrugs.

Gymnastics with groceries is her morning dance,
Dodging cart collisions, she takes every chance.
"Oops, sorry!" she chuckles, as apples roll free,
Creating new games in her life's comedy spree.

Bedtime mayhem, oh what a fun fight,
Tales turn to giggles, and dreams take to flight.
A strong heart beats loud in the thrum of the night,
While chaos spins tales that twinkle and ignite.

With love as her anchor and joy as her map,
She dives into each day, without a single nap.
In a world built on laughter, she plays her own part,
With strength in her spirit and glee in her heart.

The Story Within the Silence

In the hush of the night, a ruckus begins,
As kids make up stories, where everyone wins.
The whispers of giggles bring comfort and light,
In the stories we share, the silence feels right.

A pause for reflection, then peals of delight,
As "knock-knock" jokes bounce like stars in the night.
In the cracks of the quiet, laughter's a sound,
With joy as the treasure, in silence it's found.

Through the warmth of the embraces and soft, gentle grins,
Are tales of adventure where every heart spins.
Though moments are fleeting, and times may seem grim,
In the pause of those stories, the fabric grows thin.

From the echoes of laughter to cuddles so tight,
The stories we nurture create purest delight.
In whispers and giggles, the silence takes shape,
For every heart knows there's magic in drape.

Echoes of Sacrifice

In the dance of the hours, chaos knows her name,
Stepping on Legos, yet never feels shame.
With coffee in hand and a smile from ear to ear,
She finds joy in the madness, no reason to fear.

The echoes of bedtime are sweetened with fun,
As socks march like soldiers, each battle's not won.
Her heart's made of patience, with a dash of delight,
Forging memories gold in the soft evening light.

As crumbs follow her footsteps like loyal little friends,
The tales told at supper are where laughter transcends.
Amidst the messiness, love glimmers bright,
In every little sacrifice, is a pure heart's light.

Through echoes of giggles and occasional tears,
She spins every moment, unfazed by her years.
With a wink and a nudge, each day she unpacks,
The joys of her journey in a life that's unwrapped.

Roads to Recovery

When bumps in the road are simply a sneeze,
She dodges and weaves with enviable ease.
A superhero cape made of old paper towels,
She navigates messes, while laughter just howls.

In a world of recovery and sticky situations,
She finds the bright side in every frustration.
With glue and some giggles, she crafts a new tale,
As hearts find their rhythm, and laughter sets sail.

With each little setback, there's always a prank,
A tickle to laughter, the joy in the tank.
Compassion her compass, she leads with a grin,
In roads full of laughter, the love spirals in.

In her heart every moment is precious and grand,
With messy adventures that never go bland.
Through recovery's journey, she thrives on the cheer,
For every road taken, she's got laughter near.

Tender Hands

With Band-Aids and snacks in my trusty backpack,
I navigate chaos, no plan to unpack.
Spilled juice and giggles, a wild ballet,
I'm a circus performer, come what may.

Hands on my hips, I survey the scene,
Crayons on walls, is this art or obscene?
With a laugh and a shrug, I embrace the mess,
It's all part of love, I suppose, I guess.

Juggling the toys, I'm a pro, can't you tell?
Setting the stage for a toddler's hard sell.
"Just one more cookie?" they plead with big eyes,
Who knew dessert could sound like sweet lies?

With stories at night, I'm a magical guide,
In a world filled with dragons, it's joy that we ride.
So here's to the moments, both silly and grand,
In this whirl of laughter, I take my stand.

Gentle Heart

In a world of noise, I wear my soft shield,
With hugs and giggles, my armor is revealed.
Sips of warm cocoa, laughter on the air,
Mismatched socks, but who has a care?

"Why's the sky blue?" they ask with pure glee,
I search for the answer, from A to Z.
A handbook of wisdom, that's nicely misplaced,
But their smiles keep me in a happy embrace.

I serve up my patience, with extra in store,
Wiping down chaos, oh what a chore!
Yet in every stumble, we dance and we play,
I'd not trade these moments, come what may.

When bedtime arrives, it's a wild little fight,
With tales of brave heroes to drift off to light.
Though tangled in covers, there's love all around,
In the realm of the heart, laughter's profound.

Silent Sacrifice

Whispers of duty, beneath the loud brawl,
I'm the ninja of chores, who did what, and all.
They don't see my cape, but I'm soaring right here,
In the silence of laughter, I steer clear.

Sneaking in veggies, in cookies they bake,
A mom's secret mission, for health's little sake.
Yet every bite taken, I do a small dance,
Who knew a green bean could have such a chance?

The laundry may tower like mountains of fluff,
But I wear my smile, and that's plenty enough.
For every small task, there's giggles galore,
I skedaddle through chaos, then sneak for some more.

And when it gets quiet, they're plotting new schemes,
I snicker and listen, their wild little dreams.
In this hidden ballet of laughter and care,
I glide through the chaos, with joy to spare.

Whispers of Compassion

In a land of lost socks, and tangled up toys,
I'm the keeper of giggles and sweet little joys.
With a dab of glue, and a sprinkle of cheer,
I'm the fairy of comfort, let's make it clear.

Oh, the tales they spin, with bright shining eyes,
About monsters and aliens in playful disguise.
I nod and I smile, totally bought in,
Who knew caring hearts could wear such a grin?

On rainy days, we build forts with great might,
From pillows and blankets, we conquer the night.
With popcorn for treasure, and stories stacked high,
We're pirates on ships, brave hearts in the sky.

In the whirlwind of chaos, compassion will dance,
With each little moment, we give it a chance.
In laughter and love, we find our own spark,
In this beautiful journey, I leave my mark.

Threads of Comfort

With each tangled knot, I weave in some fun,
Sewing up memories, our threads tightly spun.
A trip to the zoo? Oh, what a delight!
I'm the jester and guide, through our magical night.

"Can we tame a lion?" they shout with pure glee,
I chuckle and say, "Only if you're free!"
In the fabric of life, every stitch tells a tale,
Of bravery, mischief, and laughter we hail.

Baking disasters, a cake made of goo,
Yet smiles are the icing, as sweet as the view.
With mishaps and mayhem, we dance in the light,
Creating our treasures, oh, what a sight!

In the tapestry woven, our fibers entwined,
There's warmth in the chaos, love that's defined.
With each little thread, we'll craft our own art,
In the quilt of our journey, we capture the heart.

Guardian Angels in Scrubs

In hallways bright with chatter,
They shuffle, fit to burst,
With coffee cups and laughter,
A dose of love, not just a nurse.

They juggle charts and swift goodbyes,
With humor sharp and wise,
"Call the doc, it's all a hoax!"
They quip as laughter fills the skies.

Stethoscopes a-dangerous tease,
Tickling ribs with ease,
With every sigh and laugh they share,
They mend hearts, as if it's a breeze.

So here's to them, our silly crew,
In scrubs of every hue,
Through giggles, hugs, and silly pranks,
They make us feel brand new!

The Unseen Canvas

In a room of calm despair,
Creativity fills the air,
With crayons, paints, and silly hats,
They craft a world beyond our cares.

Each brushstroke tells a tale,
With giggles mixed in the female,
While glue sticks and glitter glide,
Creating happiness without fail.

They harness joy like windswept kites,
Transforming fears into delights,
With every stroke, a chuckle shared,
Turning moments into flights.

In art room chaos, magic flows,
As laughter roars and creativity grows,
Painting smiles where pain once lurked,
An unseen canvas that brightly glows.

Bonds in the Aftermath

In the wake of stormy nights,
They gather close to share their rights,
With stories spun of wild and woe,
In warmth like cocoa, they find their sights.

They've seen it all, the highs and lows,
With friendship blooming like garden grows,
Bonds forged in laughter and the tears,
As hope through the uncertainty flows.

"Remember the time?" a voice rings clear,
Shared snickers mixed with heartfelt cheer,
In every mishap, every blend,
They dance, a little wobbly, near.

With jokes that lighten, blessings sent,
In every moment, a giggle lent,
Together stitched in love's embrace,
In aftermaths, where joy's intent.

Heartbeats and Healing Hands

In rhythm with each fragile heart,
They waltz like dancers, a work of art,
With healing hands and gentle grace,
They bring the smiles back to the chart.

A touch, a poke, a silly joke,
With every shift, they break the yoke,
Heartbeats resonate, a funny dance,
Through care and cheer, their way they stoke.

Nurses laugh with every task,
While patients giggle, "What's the ask?"
In laughter's ease, a bond emerges,
A world transformed behind each mask.

So let's applaud their tender toil,
In moments shared where laughter boils,
With every pulse and joyful jest,
They craft a world where love uncoils.

The Unseen Labor of Love

In the kitchen, pots clank loud,
A meal for three, I'm quite the proud.
Juggling spoons, the cat looks on,
Baking chaos from dusk till dawn.

Laundry piles make a mountain peak,
Socks on the left, the right's gone meek.
Found a rogue crayon in a shirt,
Magic wash, now it's mildly hurt.

Time to play the hide and seek,
Where's the remote? Oh, what a freak!
Under the couch, a few old fries,
When did this turn into a prize?

With laughter, the mess, I'll embrace,
Every mishap, a funny face.
In a world where love's never brief,
We find our joy through silly grief.

Lanterns Along the Path

Stumbling through toys, I start to laugh,
Tripping over the big stuffed calf.
Lanterns lit by giggles and cheer,
In this maze, my heart feels near.

Follow the trail of crumbs and socks,
Each twist and turn, oh what a paradox!
Under the covers, secrets we share,
Silly stories float in the air.

Tales of dragons and heroic deeds,
Hiding my grin, fulfilling their needs.
With each shadow dancing on the wall,
I ring the bell for the evening call.

So here we roam, lanterns aglow,
Finding our way, with love in tow.
Every stumble, a joyful misstep,
In this adventure, our hearts adept.

Heartstrings Intertwined

Waking up to 'Mom' and 'Dad' calls,
In pajamas that are far from small.
We're tied together with splattered paint,
Messy art, like a saint's complaint.

Dance parties break out in the hall,
Socks on the floor, we might just fall.
Childhood laughter rings through the air,
With every twirl, I shed my despair.

Wobbly knees and ice cream stains,
Chasing butterflies in silly gains.
Their scrunched-up faces, a comedic sight,
In this tangled love, life feels just right.

Heartstrings pull in angles quite bizarre,
Our family car's a quirky bazaar.
Every journey, a wild ride,
With love and laughter as our guide.

Serenity in Shadows

When the day ends and night creeps in,
Silence wraps us like a gentle spin.
Snore symphonies from the kids' room,
In the chaos, peace starts to bloom.

I tiptoe softly, avoiding the creaks,
Laughing at memories that make me weak.
Stars twinkle bright through the window's guard,
In this stillness, I take a yard.

A mug of tea, my only friend,
Dreams of escape, just around the bend.
Curtains flutter with a soft embrace,
In shadows, comfort finds its place.

Every giggle from the room next door,
Reminds me why I adore this chore.
For even in quiet, the humor reigns,
Serenity found in love's sweet chains.

Comfort in the Chaos

In the middle of the mess, kids shout and play,
Spilled milk on the floor, oh, what a day!
Yet laughter fills the air, in a joyful burst,
We dance through the chaos, quenching our thirst.

Mismatched socks and toys everywhere,
Dinner's a circus, we laugh, if you dare!
Peas on the ceiling and laughter that rings,
What chaos brings joy; oh, the joy that it sings!

Chasing small feet through rooms full of dreams,
Every day's lesson is not what it seems.
With playful chaos, a grin on each face,
In this wacky world, we find our own place.

So here's to the laughter that fills up our home,
With spills and with giggles, we freely roam.
In comfort found strangely, in all of this mess,
There's love in the chaos; we couldn't love less!

The Art of Unseen Labor

You think that I'm idle, just standing and waiting,
But magic is brewing while pot pans are dating.
I'm an artist with laundry, a master of stew,
My canvas is chaos, and my muse is you!

Each sock that is folded, each crayon in place,
A treasure map hidden, a game of base chase.
Who knew that a dish would inspire great lore?
Or a stubborn stain could spark giggles galore?

The broom is my wand, with a swish and a sweep,
Transforming our floors from your wild jump and leap.
While you're off on adventures, carefree through the day,

I'm here making magic in my own special way.

So cheers to the labor that's often unseen,
To the smiles and the giggles, the glorious green!
The art of the mundane, it deserves a grand cheer,
For behind every moment, there's fun to be near!

Holding the Light

In the hallway I stumble, a toy on my toes,
Stumbling and mumbling, my balance just goes.
But each little giggle, it lights up the dark,
Like fireflies dancing, igniting the spark.

The nightly routine is a theatrical play,
With bedtime stories that lead us astray.
I hold up the flashlight, a beacon of hope,
As monsters are vanquished, we learn how to cope.

With blankets and pillows, we create our own fort,
Imagination takes flight, in our little resort.
The whispers of dreams are what carry us high,
As love in the dark adds a soft lullaby.

So here's to the moments, both silly and sweet,
To giggles at shadows and imaginary feats.
In holding the light, we find joy in the night,
As love shines the brightest, making everything right!

Unraveled Threads

Look at this sweater, once warm and so neat,
Now a patchwork of colors, it's stuck on repeat.
Countless adventures have frayed all the seams,
But laughter's the needle that stitches our dreams.

I juggle the rest as clothes drift away,
Each shirt tells a story of laughable fray.
The dryer's a portal to childhood delight,
Where socks go to party, oh what a night!

We take on the tangles, the twists and the spins,
Finding joy in the chaos, where friendship begins.
Each mess is a treasure, a sign of the play,
An artwork of fibers from our wild day.

So here's to unraveling with humor and cheer,
To the threads of our lives that hold love so near.
In this funky creation, with colors that blend,
We find joy in the messy; it's fun without end!

Pages of Patience

In a world of spills and endless fuss,
Dancing to the tune of a toddler's bus.
I count to ten while dodging toys,
And laugh through chaos with my noisy joys.

Cookies crumbled in my pockets tight,
Chasing giggles into the night.
Bandaids on knees, a superhero cape,
Life's sweet circus, with no escape!

Balancing snacks on my head with grace,
Mismatched socks, still I embrace.
Time ticks slowly, but laughter thrives,
In patience pages, the joy derives.

Gentle Remedies

A spoonful of sugar and a pinch of cheer,
Now, where's that cough syrup? Oh, it's here!
With band-aids and kisses, I patch up the strife,
Mixing a potion—oh, what a life!

Socks on the cat, a quick little prank,
I'll play the fool, yes, that's my rank.
Lemonade magic, a twist of the wrist,
With humor in hand, none could resist.

I juggle requests in a wild show,
From ice packs to pancakes, on the go.
Each day a remedy, quirky and fun,
Not a single moment dull under the sun!

Stories of Sacrifice

Tales of bedtime, oh what a sight,
Trading my pillow for another goodnight.
I read of dragons and knights with pride,
While stifling yawns, as the stories collide.

Sacrifice sounds so noble, so grand,
But wait 'til you see how the laundry's planned.
For every lost toy and every late meal,
There's laughter and love in the deal!

With every tantrum, a rainbow appears,
Melted crayons turned into cheers.
For every sacrifice, a giggle erupts,
In this wild tale where joy corrupts!

Reminders in the Routine

Morning chaos, finding my shoes,
Chasing my coffee while dodging the snooze.
In sticky routines, I set the tone,
With dance moves that make my heart feel at home.

Lists on the fridge like art on display,
A gentle reminder to seize the day.
"Remember the snacks!" I chant with flair,
In my goofy rhythm, I twirl without care.

Homework battles and dinner fights,
All the while raising my bar, reaching new heights.
Routine so absurd, yet golden with glee,
In each silly moment, pure jubilee!

A Symphony of Selflessness

In a world full of mess, I take the lead,
Balancing life, with laughter indeed.
Spilled soup on my shirt, I laugh it away,
Juggling more tasks than there are in a play.

When socks go missing, I don't lose my cool,
I just claim it's a game; it's the new 'lost school'.
Dance with a broom, let the dust bunnies spin,
I'll clean up this chaos, let the chaos begin!

A band of unruly little feet run about,
Each sound like a drum, instilling some doubt.
But through all the chaos, much joy's in the mix,
High-fiving my plants, who are tangled in tricks.

So here's to the laughter, every silly slip,
We waltz through the mishaps, holding joy as our grip.
In this comical dance we twirl and we sway,
I'm a maestro of mayhem; let's cheer for the play!

The Quiet Rescue

In the library hush, I whisper a plea,
Where silence is golden, not for you or for me.
A snack cup is missing, the culprit in sight,
Frantically searching in the dimmest of light.

Oh, the stealth of a shadow, the sneak of a snack,
Creeping through cushions, I'm on the right track.
But that giggle erupts, I know who to blame,
A toddler with crumbs, can't quite play it the same.

The hero emerges, with juice box in hand,
Supervised chaos, it's all going as planned.
I sip on my coffee, they slosh all around,
This rescue is sweet—messy joy is profound.

In moments like these, quiet bliss is a joke,
With laughter the only weapon, we're ready to poke.
Together we'll conquer, each hurdle we face,
In this quiet rescue, I've found my true place!

Whispers Across the Room

A look shared in silence, it sparks something fun,
With rolled eyes and giggles, our battle begun.
Sneaking past chores for a quick little treat,
The mission's a riot, though it's not quite discreet.

Whispers of ice cream, betraying our fate,
With sticky fingers, it's a sugar-filled state.
Tiptoeing softly, like ninjas at play,
While the laundry piles high, we play our own way.

Between all the whisperings, laughter erupts,
From hiding bad snacks to mischief that erupts.
Every crumb we collect is a badge of our cheer,
In this circus we thrive, there's no room for a fear.

So let our secrets flutter like sweet little blooms,
In the heart of this chaos, I welcome the zooms.
Embracing the laughter, in whispers we meet,
In this magical moment, joy tastes like a treat!

Traces of Trust

With crayons on walls, oh what a delight,
A masterpiece crafted in the middle of night.
Chasing down giggles between every twist,
With faces of mischief, oh, how can I resist?

Sticky fingerprints mark every door,
As I navigate puddles and crumbs on the floor.
Tucking in laughter like stars in a jar,
Traces of trust lead us both very far.

Through tattered old books, we chart out our quest,
Each story a treasure, we're simply the best.
In pillow forts made, where explorers ignite,
The laughter is blazing, our spirits take flight.

So here we will wander, through sunsets and beams,
With giggles as anchors, we'll sail on our dreams.
In this world of our making, each joy we'll assess,
Traces of trust will forever impress!

Echoes in the Quiet

In a house where silence reigns,
A sneeze gets all the attention.
Cats make better choices,
While I make the next misstep.

Laughter spills like milk,
Slippers go on the wrong feet.
Careful, there's a puddle here,
But no one sees my defeat.

Jelly stains on the wallpaper,
Spaghetti sauce on the floor,
With every tiny disaster,
I find a bit more to adore.

The radio plays old tunes,
But I dance the wayward jig.
Mom's comfort's got a rhythm,
And a slightly offbeat gig.

Nurturing the Wounds

I patch up knees every day,
With band-aids shaped like fish.
Turns out, they wear it proudly,
'Til bedtime, it's a wild wish.

Ice cream helps with the scrapes,
Each scoop a magic potion.
Wounds heal with giggle fits,
And a playful, dreamy motion.

Chocolate smudge on my cheek,
Is it mine or from the kid?
Together we're a mess,
Yet laughter always wins, we did!

Beyond the Bandage

Beyond the hugs and kisses,
Is a world of little spies.
They track my every move,
With watchful, gleaming eyes.

I'm the secret agent now,
With snacks as my disguise.
Subterfuge with gummy bears,
Who knew that would be wise?

Rambunctious little rebels,
They tear through the day with glee.
And me, their sly commander,
Waving crayons as my key!

A Tapestry of Time

In this quilt of everyday,
We stitch with joy and sighs.
Each patch a tiny moment,
Of chaos masked by our highs.

Cupcakes turn into laughter,
And tantrums fade away.
With a wink and silly dance,
I find life's a playful play.

So we gather all our nights,
Under stars and silly dreams.
Every stitch tells a story,
Of love stitched at the seams.

In the Shadows of Healing

In the corner, a band-aid fights,
As I wrestle with stubborn small bites.
Laughter erupts from a sneeze gone wrong,
Who knew that healing could feel so strong?

A rubber chicken brings joy to the scene,
As I clean up the mess from my little green machine.
With giggles and gripes, the day rolls ahead,
Healing's a circus, and I'm the one fed!

Plasters and potions on every shelf,
We're just one step away from a mischievous elf.
With laughter and chaos, we mend every ache,
A spoonful of fun is the best kind of shake!

In the shadows where care often hides,
Funny tales grow where kindness resides.
Join me for a laugh, that's what we'll do,
In this lively dance of healing, it's me and you!

Embracing the Wounded

A hug from a crutch, oh what a twist,
Who knew support came with a comedic list?
We juggle with bandages, laughter on cue,
In a world built of giggles, we heal and renew.

Tickles from tablets, who knew they could sing?
They dance to a rhythm, like a springy old spring.
The wounded embrace with pots and a pan,
In this kitchen of care, there's always a plan!

In the great game of patience, I redirect,
Socks on the roof become the main project.
Laughter's the glue that holds it all tight,
Turning wounds into stories, all day and night!

So let's celebrate chaos, it's all that we've got,
With hugs and some humor, we'll dance on the spot.
Together we're stronger, let's give it a try,
In this playful embrace, we can reach for the sky!

From Burden to Blessing

In the early hours, spoonfuls are tossed,
While cereal wars leave few straws uncrossed.
A spill turns to laughter, our morning delight,
Turns burdens to blessings in morning light.

Pillows become forts in our playful retreat,
As battles of laughter echo through the street.
Who needs a worry when we've got our crew?
In this circus of life, there's much more to do!

From fumbles to mishaps, with grace we'll glide,
Each step a new journey, let's take it in stride.
With every chuckle, the burdens won't win,
For laughter's our armor, and joy's tucked within!

So let's lift each other, join hands in the fray,
From burden to blessing, we'll dance all day.
With smiles in abundance and hearts oh so light,
We'll treasure this journey, shining ever bright!

Echoes of Nurture

In a world full of echos, we twist and contort,
Finding joy in the moments, like a well-timed sport.
A sneeze, a laugh—that's the game we play,
Turning echoes to giggles, day after day.

With jokes on our lips and care in our hearts,
We gather the pieces, piecing up arts.
In this patchwork of healing, we find our own role,
Laughter's the language that helps make us whole.

In the hallway of memories, silly sounds chime,
Each echo a heartbeat, with rhythm and rhyme.
We dance through the trials with grace and a grin,
In this celebration of laughter, let's all join in!

So echo, dear friend, these moments we share,
Who knew that this journey could be so rare?
With whimsy and wonder, let's nurture the fun,
In the echoes of laughter, we've already won!

www.ingramcontent.com/pod-product-compliance
Lightning Source LLC
Chambersburg PA
CBHW070312120526
44590CB00017B/2648